PRAYERS
OF
DELIVERANCE
AND
DECREES

ACCESSING THE AUTHORITY OF THE NAME, THE WORD, THE BLOOD, AND THE CROSS OF CHRIST

TERESA VERDECCHIO

PRAYERS OF DELIVERANCE & DECREES
© 2022 Teresa Verdecchio.

Published by Teresa Verdecchio | Downington, PA

ISBN (Paperback): 978-1-7352777-6-9

Printed in the United States of America

Prepared for Publication: www.wendykwalters.com

Scripture quotations marked KJV are taken from the *King James Version* of the Bible and are in the public domain.

Scripture quotations marked AMP are taken from *The Amplified® Bible*, Copyright © 1954, 1958, 1962, 1964, 1965, 1987 by The Lockman Foundation. Used by permission. (www.Lockman.org)

To contact the author: www.newdestinychristiancenter.com

DEDICATION

This book is dedicated to my grandsons, Carson David Juristy and Gunnar Reece Juristy. May freedom be your legacy!

THANK YOU

A special thank you to Doug Kennedy and Lisa Verdecchio for all your help editing my prayers for this project. A heartfelt thank you to Wendy Walters, the greatest cover designer and author coach. Thanks for jumping in and adding your flair.

FOREWORD

The battle between good and evil, God and Satan, is old and visible, especially now. Like a natural war, there are prisoners in the kingdom of darkness. There are people that have been freed from the devil by the power of the cross, however due to demonic captivity there have been strongholds built in their minds from memories of pain, rejection, and shame.

These strongholds can build a cyclical pattern of feelings of failure and discouragement. In the book of Ephesians 4:23, this issue is addressed, "Be renewed in the spirit of your mind."

Deliverance from demonic power was a regular part of Jesus' ministry. He did it and instructed His disciples to do the same. However, He never set anyone free against their will. The freedom to choose is protected by God in Scripture.

"I call heaven and earth to record this day against you, that I have set before you life and death, blessing and cursing:

therefore choose life, that both thou and thy seed may live" (Deuteronomy 30:19).

Jesus Himself in Luke 22:42 prayed to do the will of God so His will would be aligned with God's will, "Saying, Father, if thou be willing, remove this cup from me: nevertheless not my will, but thine, be done."

The will of God was to go to the cross and suffer so men could be freed from demonic power (1 John 3:8).

Like Jesus, the power to change as Christians begins with prayer. In the pages of this book there are prayers that give God access to your situation.

By praying, you will receive the grace (God's ability) to do what seemed impossible. By priming the pump of prayer you will create a series of victories in your life and build momentum against demonic power.

May these prayers bring you the freedom that God has planned for you.

—JOE PEROZICH
Founding Apostle of MFC Ministries
www.mfcministries.net

AUTHOR'S NOTE

It is my desire that these prayers of deliverance and decrees from the Word of God will bless and assist you as you echo God's authority and dominion in your life through the Name, the Word, the Blood, and the Cross of Jesus.

> "I love the LORD, because He has heard
> my voice and my pleas for mercy."
>
> PSALM 116:1

I pray that every bondage is broken and every wound is healed as you journey on in victory and freedom. Now go, live an EPIC life!

—TERESA VERDECCHIO
Founder/President of EPIC Women
Pastor, Counselor, Author

CONTENTS

PRAYERS OF DELIVERANCE/CONSECRATION   12
SELF   13
LUST   14
WILL   15
PURIFICATION/HOLINESS   16
HEALING AND EMOTIONAL STABILITY   17
IDENTITY   18
PROSPERITY   19
CLOSE FELLOWSHIP   20
FEAR   21
MIND   22
PATIENCE   23
INNER HEALING   24
RELEASING THE KINGDOM   25
PRODIGALS   26
INTERCESSION FOR LOST LOVED ONES   27
BLESSINGS OVER CHILDREN   28
EMOTIONAL HEALING   30
HOME   32
BREAKING CURSES   34
WITCHCRAFT   35
DELIVERANCE FROM EATING DISORDERS   36
OFFENSE AND INJUSTICE   37
BREAKING GENERATIONAL CURSES   38
RELATIONSHIPS   39
RESISTING THE DEVIL   40
SELF   41

SECRETS	42
SOUND MIND	43
TAMING THE TONGUE	44
TONGUE	45
REPENTANCE FOR INDEPENDENCE AND PRIDE	46
RELEASE FROM GUILT AND SHAME	47
PASSIVITY	48
GODLY FRIENDSHIPS	50
LOVE WALK	52
CONSECRATION	53
ADDRESSING TORMENT ON MY CHILDREN	54
BREAKING THE POWER OF LIES	55
BOLD WITNESS	56
TRANSPARENCY	57
REPENTANCE	58
THANKFULNESS FOR SALVATION	60
MOVING INTO THE PROMISED LAND	61
SEXUAL IMMORALITY	62
PRAYER FOR FINANCES	64
PRAYER OF SALVATION	67
MORE RESOURCES	68

POSTURED IN VICTORY

Father, I come delightfully close to You by the blood of the Lord Jesus Christ. I humble myself and by faith, I apply the precious blood of Jesus over my spirit, soul and body, over my past, present and future days. I apply the blood of Jesus over the work of my hands and my ministry, over my coming and going, over the door post of my life, over me and mine, over my possessions, over my health, and over my wealth. I apply the blood of the Lord Jesus Christ over everything pertaining to me. I break off any and all demonic attachments from any person, place, or thing that I associated with. I put the cross of the Lord Jesus Christ between myself and those that I interact with. I bind any demonic interference and I forbid any demon from placing upon me lies, thoughts, and emotions contrary to another person and I bind any demon from placing upon them any lies, thoughts, and emotions contrary to me. I declare that I live at peace with those around me in the name of Jesus.

PRAYERS OF DELIVERANCE/ CONSECRATION

Father, I ask in Jesus' name that You would align everything on the inside of me to everything on the inside of You, and that my thoughts and my desires would be Your thoughts and desires. May I be aligned with your throne of grace.

Father, I ask that you consecrate me wholly—spirit, soul, and body. Remove anything from within me that is not loyal to You. Forgive me and cleanse me of my idols. (1 John 5:21)

> Little children, keep yourselves from idols (false gods) – [from anything and everything that would occupy the place in your heart due to God, from any sort of substitute from Him that would take place in your life.] Amen. (So let it be.)
>
> 1 JOHN 5:21 (AMP)

SELF

Father, I repent for the sin of independence. Forgive me for every tendency within to strike out on my own journey independent of You. God, please do not allow me to do anything independent of You. Forgive me for relying on my own ways of thinking and for doing my own thing. Forgive me for trying to succeed outside of You. I bring before You my self-sufficiency and I ask that Calvary's tree would come down on me and set me free. I repent of my controlling ways and any tug-of-war that ensues between myself and Your will. I surrender. I give You my life. Consecrate me, sanctify me, and set me apart for Your plan. May I become agreeable to Your will.

LUST

Father, I bind the lust of the flesh, the lust of the eyes, and pride of life in the name of Jesus. (1 John 2:16). Keep me from the spirit of the world. Keep me loyal unto You – loving You with all of my heart, mind, soul, and strength (Mark 12:30).

WILL

Father, in the name of Jesus, I bind my will to the will of Father-God. Not my will, but Your will be done (Luke 22:42). I bind my mind to the mind of Christ, for I've been given the mind of Christ and now hold His thoughts, feelings, and intents (1 Corinthians 2:16). I bind my emotions to the Holy Spirit.

PURIFICATION/HOLINESS

Father, You said that there is a Highway of Holiness and that no unclean thing shall step upon it (Isaiah 35:8). I ask that You would keep me from falling into the ditches of uncleanness on the right and on the left, that You would purify me of any and all unclean things. Father, I repent of the unclean thing: I repent of sexual immorality. I repent of gossip, strife, bitterness, hatred, and racism. I repent of envy, jealousy and pride. I renounce these sins and I command them to leave me along with every demonic influence.

I pray that I would be submitted to, controlled by, and led by the Holy Spirit. I pray that I would be under His influence. I pray that I would have an appetite for holy things, for godly things, and for decent things. In Jesus' name, Amen.

HEALING AND EMOTIONAL STABILITY

I speak over my body and I declare in the name of Jesus that chemical balance comes to my brain, that every organ, system, tissue and cell in my body is aligned with the Word of God that declares that by the stripes of Jesus I was healed (1 Peter 2:24). I speak emotional stability to my emotions. I say that I am sturdy and stable in my emotions. I say that I have emotions that are submitted to the Holy Spirit. I bind my emotions to the Holy Spirit. Holy Spirit, You are the riverbanks and my emotions do not exceed those godly boundaries. I confess I have self-control and temperance in the name of Jesus.

IDENTITY

I am the righteousness of God in Christ Jesus (2 Corinthians 5:21). I have been made right with Father-God because of what Jesus did for me (Romans 3:24). Thank You Jesus for shedding Your blood for me and giving me peace with Father-God (Romans 5:1). Thank You that I have access and I can come in boldly to my Father's presence, free of fear, inferiority, shame, and condemnation. I come in not hanging my head low, but I come in as a child (daughter/son) of the Most High God. I come with joy. I come with expectation. I come with anticipation.

My Father loves to fellowship with me and I love to fellowship with Him. I delight to do Your will and I feed upon Your faithfulness. I am an overcomer by the blood of the Lamb and the word of my testimony (Revelation 12:11). I am the righteousness of God in Christ Jesus. I can do all things through Christ who strengthens me (Philippians 4:13).

PROSPERITY

The blessings of Abraham, Isaac, and Jacob are upon my life. I prosper coming in and I prosper going out. I prosper in the country and I prosper in the city (Deuteronomy 28:3).

God gives me favorable business deals. He brings real estate to me. I bind the deed of the property to my name. Thank You that I own everything, that I am a lender and not a borrower (Deuteronomy 28:12). I worship You in the place called "done." Thank You Jesus for everything you did to make Your Father my Father. I'm so thankful and I give You praise with thanksgiving.

CLOSE FELLOWSHIP

Father, I come to You humbly because I can come to You boldly. I ask for a greater level of fellowship with You. I ask for unbroken and abiding fellowship. I ask that You teach me, Holy Spirit, how to walk circumspectly and how to obey the principles of God. I ask that You would give me good success as you impart your wisdom to me to enter into those places.

FEAR

Father, in the name of Jesus I take authority over the spirit of fear and I cast it out. Your Word says that perfect love casts out fear, because fear involves torment (1 John 4:18). I cast it out and away from me in the name of Jesus, with all of its manifestations of panic attacks, anxiety attacks, fear, phobias, and nightmares in the name of the Lord Jesus Christ. Loose my emotions. Loose my nervous system. Loose my imaginations. Loose my memories. I speak healing over my body and every way that it's been terrorized by the enemy. I speak health to all my systems in the name of the Lord Jesus Christ for by Your stripes Jesus I was healed (1 Peter 2:21-25). I thank You for the manifestation of Your healing in my body.

MIND

Father, I thank You that I have the mind of Christ (1 Corinthians 2:16). I have a powerful, loving, sound, calm, well balanced, authoritative, and self-controlled mind. I access, possess, and hold the thoughts of Christ Jesus. My mind thinks in orderly ways. I am able to retrieve information. I have rapid recall. My mind serves the mind of the Spirit. I access the mind of Christ. My mind has a winning attitude. I'm an overcomer by the blood of the Lamb and the word of my testimony. I am the head and not the tail. I am above and not beneath (Deut. 28:13). The Lord God goes before me and gives me good success (2 Samuel 23:5). He teaches me how to meditate upon His words and I am a success in the Kingdom of God. I have thoughts that are orderly and not chaotic. I declare that I am a problem solver and not a problem causer.

PATIENCE

Father, I thank You that by faith and patience I do possess the promises (Hebrews 6:12). I drive out impatience, which is the fruit of pride in the mighty name of Jesus. I will learn to wait upon the Lord and I will rest in His goodness. I will be satisfied as I feed upon His faithfulness (Psalm 37:3-4). I thank You that I open my mouth and You fill it with good things. I do taste and see that the Lord is good (Psalm 34:8). Thank You for Your goodness and kindness. Thank You for Your mercy for my life. Thank You that You condescend to me and You bring Your goodness and Your faithfulness over my life.

INNER HEALING

Father, I thank You in the name of Jesus that Your love comes and overwhelms places of inferiority and insecurity deep on the inside of me. I thank You that Your love heals me of every wound, every hurt, and every place that the enemy has shot his poisonous, bitter arrows. I break rejection off my life and I confront it for the lie that it is, for I am accepted in Christ Jesus. I am accepted in the Beloved (Ephesians 1:6). I thank You that I am loved and adored. I thank You that I was worth the price of the blood of Your Son. I am of great value and I am a great treasure to heaven. From this day forward, I will not believe the lies of rejection. When I feel insecure, I will take a moment and pause in Your presence and receive greater amounts of Your love which makes me secure in my identity.

RELEASING THE KINGDOM

I take authority over this atmosphere in the name of Jesus and I declare and decree that wherever I go the Kingdom of God goes—the Kingdom of righteousness, peace, and joy in the Holy Ghost (Romans 14:17). I bind every devil and I loose the angels of God to go before me and to make a way where there seems to be no way (Isaiah 43:19). Father I thank You that the angels clear the pathway, that I walk forward Father God free of fear, free of terror, and that there is no harm or evil that can come upon me in the name of Jesus.

I bind every devil (Matthew 18:19), everything that was devised in the council room of hell—I break it, I take authority over it, and I abort it in the realm of the spirit before it has expression and manifestation in the natural in the name of Jesus. I loose the power and the presence of God and the ministering spirits of the angels to come and minister to this heir of salvation (Hebrews 1:14). Thank You that no weapon formed against me prospers (Isaiah 54:17).

PRODIGALS

Father, I lift before Your throne of grace every prodigal. I say come home in the name of Jesus. Allow their spirit to be awakened. Speak to them in dreams and visions oh God. Hover over them. Let the Spirit of the Lord rush upon them. Remind them of Your goodness and faithfulness. Open their ears that they would hear the Spirit of God calling them in the night hour. Father, let them not run from You, but Lord let them run straight into Your arms of mercy and grace. Father, remove their heart of stone and give them a heart of flesh (Ezekiel 36:26). Call them. Open their ears and let them hear (Mark 4:9). Let the blinders fall from their eyes. Let the scales be removed. Release the POWs out of the enemy's camp. Father God go up and get back what is Yours in the devil's camp. I plead the blood of Jesus over them. Keep them alive long enough God, let them figure it out. Let the mercies of the Lord come down upon them to rescue, redeem, and recover them in the name of Jesus!

INTERCESSION FOR LOST LOVED ONES

I call them saved in the spirit realm. I call them anointed of heaven to cast out demons. I call them back to their place of destiny and say that they shall fulfill their days and discover their purpose by which they were created in the name of Jesus. I call those things that be not, as though they were (Romans 4:17). I am not moved by what I see, hear, or feel, because I know God that you're able to redeem and heal to the utmost. Thank You Jesus that You go after my son and You go after my daughter and that You restore them completely. Destroy the works of the devil in their life (1 John 3:8). Cover them in the blood of Jesus and have mercy upon them. I thank You for Your mercy.

BLESSINGS OVER CHILDREN

Father, I bless my sons and daughters and say that they shall fulfill their days in the Lord. I say they are the head and not the tail. They are above and not beneath (Deuteronomy 28:13). I thank You for the uncommon favor of God that surrounds them—that You cause the angels of the Lord to protect them and keep them from harm and evil. I thank You that they shall have good success and they shall remember You all of their days.

I thank You that they are blessed. Great is the peace of my children and my grandchildren (Isaiah 54:13). I thank You that they love You, see You, and serve You with all of their hearts, minds, and souls. Father I thank you that everything they are is Yours. Their possessions are covered in the blood of Jesus and I say they are blessed coming in and blessed going out. They shall leave a legacy of faith for their generations. I thank You that their marriages are blessed, their finances are blessed, and their bodies are blessed.

Let the blessing of the Lord God come down upon them and let them provoke others to jealousy because of Your goodness. Let there be an anointing upon them that they lead souls to the Lord Jesus Christ. Let their businesses be blessed and whatever they put their hand to prosper. Great shall be the peace of my children, because they walk with the Lord.

"Beware that you do not despise or feel scornful toward
or think little of one of these little ones, for I tell you
that in heaven their angels always are in the presence of
and look upon the face of My Father Who is in heaven."

MATTHEW 18:10 (AMP)

EMOTIONAL HEALING

Father, in the name of Jesus, I speak to every hurt, every wound, and every violation. I call demonic influences out of the place of wounding. Go in the name of the Lord Jesus Christ. I loose the balm of Gilead (Jeremiah 8:22). I loose the healing power of Jesus. Come with Your blood and wash clean the wound so I can begin to heal for by Your stripes, Jesus, I was healed (1 Peter 2:24).

I speak healing to the emotions. I speak healing to the memories. I speak healing to the imagination. I command the nightmares and the night terrors to stop in the name of the Lord Jesus Christ. I drive out every unclean demonic spirit that has been attached to this wound in the name of Jesus. I ask that You heal sexual abuse, physical abuse, emotional abuse, and mental abuse in the name of Jesus, because You took the abuse for me on Calvary's tree.

I call the trauma out of my soul and my soul out of the trauma. Jesus, You did not open Your mouth against Your enemies so I could open my mouth against the enemy. So, in the mighty name of Jesus, I rebuke the enemy and every demonic influence upon my life that he perpetrated through violence and abuse. I say, "Go from me in Jesus name!" I drive you out and I ask Holy Spirit that You would come in with Your anointing that destroys the yoke of bondage (Isaiah 10:27).

I forgive those who violated me. Bring healing, freedom, and deliverance. I speak healing to emotions. I speak healing to memories. I speak that there will be no more flashbacks in the name of Jesus, but a hope and a future infused within the spirit in Jesus' name (Jeremiah 29:11).

HOME

Father, in the name of Jesus, I ask that the Holy Spirit, who is the revealer of secrets, would look throughout my house. If there is anything in my home that is ungodly that does not honor You or that has demonic attachment to it, I ask that You reveal it to me. Holy Spirit, go through every room, every corner, every drawer, and every square-inch of my house on my property and allow it to pass the test of what is godly. If there's anything that I need to get rid of, I will throw it away. I will break agreement with it. I will not try to sell it. I will not try to profit from it, but what You condemn, I condemn. I am on the side of the Lord. I will rid myself of any books, materials, and love letters -anything from the past (Acts 19:19).

Father, in the name of Jesus, I declare the blood of Jesus over my past, present, and future days. I invite the blood of Jesus over any area of my past that has not been dealt with. I declare that my past will no longer hinder me and my future.

I give You complete and total access. Holy Spirit, unhook me from anything that has me tethered to my past in the name of Jesus for I believe the Word that if any man be in Christ, he is a new creation. Old things have passed away. Behold! All things become new (2 Corinthians 5:17). Anything in my life that is rooted in the old, uproot it in the name of the Lord Jesus Christ (Jeremiah 1:10). I declare I am a child of God without a past.

Father, I speak peace into my home. I bind every demon that has come to afflict and torment and bring a spirit of strife. I bind those demons and command them to leave in the name of Jesus. Father, I turn it at the door and I plead the blood of Jesus. I ask for the presence of the Holy Spirit to come and bring peace.

BREAKING CURSES

Father, in the name of the Lord Jesus Christ I rebuke and bind up words of witchcraft, incantations, judgments, criticism, gossip, and curses spoken or prayed against me. I forgive those that are cursing me and I give it to you God to deal with. I ask that in Your mercy You would not allow any of these things to come down upon me.

WITCHCRAFT

Father, in Jesus name, I bind and rebuke words, incantations, and all witchcraft, including witch doctors, santeria, and black magic. I thank You that it has no effect on me because the curse causeless cannot come (Proverbs 26:2). I cover myself in the blood of Jesus and I thank You that You are a shield about me of glory, that You are the lifter of my head (Psalm 3:3), and that You protect me in the name of Jesus from all harm and evil. The Lord Jesus Christ rebuke you!

DELIVERANCE FROM EATING DISORDERS

Father, in the name of Jesus I rebuke every unclean spirit involved with this eating disorder. I bring you to the light of the gospel of Jesus Christ. I will not hide in sin and shame with food. I will not go to a false comforter of food, but I go to the Holy Spirit with my wounds and I pour my complaint out before Him as it says in Psalm 142. I give you my emotions, Holy Spirit, so I do not give myself to the false comfort of food. Come Holy Spirit and deal with the roots. Come lay your ax to the root (Matthew 3:10). I bind anorexia. I bind bulimia. Go from me in the name of Jesus. I call you out of my appetite! Every eating disorder and all forms of it, false control, and the sense of control—go from me in the name of the Lord Jesus Christ.

I thank You that You teach me how to honor my body and how to properly rest, nourish it, and not abuse it in the name of Jesus. I repent for abusing my body. I thank You for who the Son sets free is free indeed (John 8:36).

OFFENSE AND INJUSTICE

Father, I ask in the name of Jesus that You would help me to trust You to defend me. Help me not to defend myself, but to take a posture of humility and trust You. I ask that You would help me not to defend myself, not to retaliate, not to justify my actions, but to entrust myself to You. You said "'Vengeance is mine,' says the Lord, 'I will repay' (Hebrews 10:30)." Help me to handle unfair treatment correctly. Sanctify my response in my reactions so that I do not allow another's sins against me to cause me to sin against You.

BREAKING GENERATIONAL CURSES

I break every generational curse that is operating in my life from my father's bloodline, my mother's bloodline, all the way back to the cross of Calvary. I apply Galatians 3:13, "Cursed is everyone who hangs on a tree," and I know that Jesus hung on the tree for me, so I ask that Calvary's tree would come down on me and set me free from any and all curses. Father, I repent for the sins of my father and my mother. I ask that You forgive us for following our own way and not Your ways, let the blood of Jesus come reverse the curse and loose the blessing in Jesus' name.

RELATIONSHIPS

Father, in the name of the Lord Jesus Christ, by faith I place the cross between myself and every human relationship, and I bind the devil and forbid him from placing upon others thoughts that are contrary towards me, and upon me thoughts that are contrary toward them. I say that we have thoughts of grace and peace toward one another and we bind the devil from any kind of interference and the spirit of strife. Break off of me any attachment from any person, place, or thing I associated with, it cannot attach to me in the name of Lord Jesus Christ. I am washed in the blood and I have peace filled, loving thoughts towards people and I bless them in the name of Jesus (Romans 12:14).

RESISTING THE DEVIL

Father, You said submit to God, resist the devil, and he will flee from me (James 4:7), so I submit to You and I say, I resist the devil and all of his works, thoughts, and emotions in the name of the Lord Jesus Christ. I take every thought captive and bring it to the obedience of Christ Jesus (2 Corinthians 10:5). I bind my will to the will of Father-God, I bind my mind to the mind of Christ, and I bind my emotions to the Holy Spirit (Thessalonians 5:23).

SELF

Father, I repent for my wrong reactions when someone sins against me. I ask that you forgive me for pride and selfishness that responded rather than allowing the response to come from my new nature. I ask that You sanctify my responses and my reactions, but even more than that, I ask that You would go deep to that place where self is exalted. Bring the power of Calvary's cross down upon my life. Forgive me for the times that I've been irritated and annoyed and had attitudes with others because of their treatment of me. I repent of my pride. I confess it is sin and I break agreement with it. I ask for humility to be a cloak around me (1 Peter 5:5), that my response to another should they sin against me would be to pardon it by grace, and not to hold the record against them. I choose not to keep score, not to condemn, and not to judge, but to release, bless, and forgive (Matthew 7:1).

"Let Your steadfast love come to me, oh Lord, Your salvation according to Your promise; then shall I have an answer for him who taunts me, for I trust in Your word."

PSALM 119:41-42

SECRETS

Father, in the name of the Lord Jesus Christ I come to Your light and I expose any darkness in me. Your Word says that God is light and in Him there is no darkness at all (1 John 1:5). I realize I am only as sick as my secrets, so I bring my secrets to the light and expose them to the truth. A devil exposed is a devil defeated. Deliver me oh God!

SOUND MIND

Father, I ask that You bring to my remembrance any unconfessed sin and that You would not allow me to hide anything. I break agreement with the enemy, and I ask that the blood of Jesus would cover my mind. I thank You that no mental illness or insanity can come upon me, that there would be no break in my mind, no mental torment, and no mental illness due to unconfessed sin (Isaiah 58:12). Bind up any breaches in Jesus' name.

I break any and all generational curses from my father's blood line and my mother's blood line (Exodus 20:5), all the way back to the cross of the Lord Jesus Christ. Nothing that they struggled with can land upon me during any season of my life in the name of Jesus. I pray that You guard me and keep me from harm and evil all the days of my life. Only goodness and mercy follow me in the mighty name of Jesus (Psalm 23).

TAMING THE TONGUE

Father, let me not sin with my mouth, giving the enemy access to my life. Forgive me for any and all times I've cast off restraint with my mouth with words of judgment and criticism of others and, as a result, given the devil legal right that the swine can turn and trample me underfoot (Matthew 7:1-6). I will not throw my pearls before swine. Either I will be justified by my words or I will be condemned by my words according to Your Word (Matthew 12:37). I agree with Your Word and I break agreement with every condemning, critical, and judgmental word in the name of Jesus from off of my life and off of the lives of others. I bless others. I bless and not curse (Romans 12:14).

TONGUE

Father, I repent for the times I've judged others and criticized them and gossiped about them. Forgive me for cursing them rather than blessing them. I repent for every idle, unproductive word that has ever come forth from my mouth. I confess my sin to You and agree with Your Word that it is sin and I thank You that You're faithful and just to forgive me of my sins and to cleanse me of all unrighteousness (1 John 1:9).

Speak to me where I need to make restitution. Bring reconciliation where possible. Let forgiveness run deep within me and lavish grace and mercy upon those around me. May the law of kindness be upon my tongue (Psalm 31:26), may my conversation be courteous and may my words minister grace to those that would hear them (Ephesians 4:29). May my words bring life and lift others around me. I humbly ask that You allow the love of God that has been shed abroad within my heart by the Holy Spirit (Romans 5:5) to flow from my person unto others, bringing glory to Jesus.

REPENTANCE FOR INDEPENDENCE AND PRIDE

Father, in the name of the Lord Jesus Christ, I humble myself and I repent of my pride. I ask that You would give me a cloak of humility (1 Peter 5:5) and You would show me how to walk humbly with You, my God (Micah 6:8). I repent of my pride and all my sins of thinking, knowing, saying, and doing. I repent of any independent thought. I repent for trying to control my own life. Please do not leave me to my own devices. Please do not leave me to myself. I ask that You would be merciful and kind to me as I know so little, but I am eager to learn Your ways and Your thoughts. I ask that You forgive me for the times that I wrestle with You for control of my life and for the times I've dethroned my Savior and put myself on the throne.

I ask that You forgive me for exalting self. Jesus, may You increase in my life and may I decrease (John 3:30). Give me the grace to die daily and to pick up my cross, deny myself, and follow You—all the way out of self and into service unto You (Luke 9:23).

RELEASE FROM GUILT AND SHAME

Father, in the mighty name of Jesus, I thank You that He who knew no sin became sin for me that I might become the righteousness of God in Christ Jesus (2 Corinthians 5:21). Because Jesus was my substitute and my sacrifice, taking my place on the cross—I'll step in with faith and receive my standing with the Father that I am made righteous and holy, blameless and forgiven.

I will no longer be held hostage by shame and guilt and all of the baggage that came with a sin filled life. But I declare that I am free for who the Son sets free is free indeed and the enemy has no hold on me (John 8:32). I am no longer a slave to sin, for sin shall no longer have dominion over me (Romans 6:14). But I echo the voice of God that declares me free of condemnation and judgment (Romans 8:1).

PASSIVITY

Father, in the name of Jesus, I thank You that You break the containment of passivity off of my life. I thank You that You cause me to be a person of action, a person of responsibility. I ask that You would forgive me for shrinking back in fear and trying to stay safe by hiding in a cave of comfort. Break every containment off of my life in every area where I have been capped and concealed.

Forgive me for not showing up and reporting for duty and for action as you called me to put my hand to the plow. I decree that I shall put my hand to the plow (Luke 9:62) and I shall not ponder passivity. Break the prison of passivity off of me.

I declare that I am a person of action, that I am a person of faith. That I echo God's victory and dominion and breakthrough in my life in the name of Jesus. Forgive me for the excuse of passivity and inactivity. Father I thank You that I am a doer of the Word (James 1:22-25) and I am not deceived but I labor while it is yet day (John 9:4).

Activate any dormant area of my life. Let my obedience be swift in the areas that You call me to action. You said that I must endure hardship as a good soldier of Jesus Christ (2 Timothy 2:3-5). I thank You for an enduring grace to labor with joy and the results shall be victory and fruitfulness rather than futility in Jesus' mighty name!

GODLY FRIENDSHIPS

Father, in the name of Jesus I ask that You order my steps and bring godly friends into my life. I trust You to remove the wrong people from my life and to bring the right people into my life. I ask that You knit our hearts together around Your purpose and Your call and not codependency (Colossians 2:2). Help me to attach to people in a healthy way as I am rooted in You and as I am secure in who I am in You.

Father, I thank You that I do not look to friendships to fulfill me, but only to be an added benefit to my life because You alone fulfill me. Father, I bless my relationships and I ask that You would teach me how to have healthy relationships, how to interact in a way that is God-honoring of myself, and of the other person and conversation. Let there be a bond of unity and peace. Let there never be a sin alliance between us, but rather a unified godly purpose as we are comrades in arms for the sake of the gospel of Jesus Christ.

I ask that You would be the center and the Lord of my friendships (Proverbs 17:17). May the Holy Spirit constantly have His eyes on my relationships and adjust any area that is not fully pleasing. Please do not allow me to make any person an idol in my life, but to keep them in the proper place and that is on the altar. May the Cross of the Lord Jesus Christ always be between myself and people. May our conversations be courteous, kind and uplifting of others. May another's reputation be safe in our hands and in our keeping. May we have a relationship that is godly and God honoring of one another and others. May we have a covenant of friendship that is strengthened by the common bond of our love for You, others and for one another. In Jesus name.

LOVE WALK

Father, in the name of Jesus I thank You that the love of God has been shed abroad within my heart by the Holy Spirit (Romans 5:5). I thank You that You help me to walk in love and that I would believe the best about others, not believing any evil report. Cause me to overlook the faults of others and to see them with godly eyes and with potential. I ask that I would love well, that I would walk in love, that I would grow in love, and that I would demonstrate the agape love of Father-God (1 Corinthians 13). May it well up on the inside of me and be a supernatural grace that would move and give expression through my person.

CONSECRATION

Father, may my heart be pure and my walk be pleasing to You (Colossians 1:10). I ask that You would create in me a clean heart and renew a right and a steadfast spirit within me (Psalm 51:10). Deliver my soul from lying lips and from a deceitful tongue. May I desire what You desire, love what You love, and hate what You hate. I set my heart and my affections upon You. I give You my praise and my adoration. I open the treasures of my heart and give You my affections, my love, and my loyalty. Help me to honor You.

I pledge my allegiance to You, Jesus. Help me to never self-preserve and betray You or others. Help me to lose my life that I might find it (Mark 8:35). I give You the treasures of my heart: my love, my adoration, my affections, my praise and my worship. I pray that I would love You Lord God with all of my heart and mind and soul and strength, and love my neighbor as myself (Luke 10:27). I pray that I would bring glory and honor to you with my thoughts and with my words all of my days. Let the inclinations of my heart be pure and not evil. In Jesus' name!

ADDRESSING TORMENT ON MY CHILDREN

Father, I break off of my children any spirits that attached to them while they were away from the house. Anything from their school, their teachers, fellow students, or their surroundings. I break off every spirit that attempted to attach to them. No spirit will torment them or vex them in the name of Jesus. For I say Jesus covers my children and their peace shall be great for the favor of the Lord rests upon their life.

I pray a hedge of protection about them. Jesus, fence them in and hem them in. Release ministering angels to go before and behind and watch over them everywhere they go.

BREAKING THE POWER OF LIES

Father, Your Word says in Proverbs 23:23 to "buy the truth and sell it not." Therefore, I choose to align my belief system with the authority of Your Word. I refuse to believe the lies and I take a stand with righteousness against the lies that the world would tell me. I refuse to exchange God's truth for the lie in regard to culture, sexuality, race, and politics. Remove weakness and fear out of me that would exchange the truth for a lie. I ask that You allow the Holy Spirit to inoculate me against lies and deception. Please do not allow me to believe seducing doctrines of demons (1 Timothy 4:1), but allow me to drill down deep into the truth and to be rooted in Christ's love. Help me to love what You love and hate what You hate.

BOLD WITNESS

Father, I ask that You would anoint me to do the work of an evangelist (2 Timothy 4:5). Empower me to preach the gospel of Jesus Christ. I ask for Your heart for the lost and broken. Give me, by grace, a net to cast to lost humanity with love. Oh, that You would soften hearts and grant men and women repentance. Open their hearts and ears wide to the gospel of Jesus Christ. Remove the scales from their eyes (Psalm 119:18) and reveal the Lord Jesus to them.

TRANSPARENCY

Father, in the name of Jesus I ask that You deliver me from the things that have tried to hold me in one place, those things I have yet to discern. I pray that as I fellowship with You, You would remove the blocks of intimacy in my walk with You. I ask that You give me transparency and vulnerability as I fellowship in Your presence.

Teach me to get away from the distractions of the busyness of this life and to steal away with You and trade my time for the treasure of heaven, which is Your presence. I ask that You cause discipline and self-control to come up in me, that You would give me the wisdom for time management so that I would order my life, with Your presence as the priority. I thank You for this grace to enter in, in the name of Jesus.

REPENTANCE

Father, in the name of Jesus, I confess my sin and ask You to forgive me and cleanse me of all unrighteousness (1 John 1:9). Let the blood of Jesus wash me clean. I ask that You take the coal from the altar, touch my lips, and purge me of iniquity (Isaiah 6:7). May the words of my mouth and the meditation of my heart to be acceptable and pleasing in Your sight, oh Lord my strength and my redeemer (Psalm 19:14).

Create in me a clean heart O God, and renew a right and a steadfast spirit within me. Do not cast me out away from Your presence for I need my dear and close friend, Holy Spirit to restore to me the joy of salvation (Psalm 51:10-12). Let my heart be pure and my walk clean. Let me walk with You God and let me please You.

I ask that You open up the Word to me and give me the Spirit of wisdom and revelation and that You would enlighten me (Ephesians 1:17). Show me the mysteries God. Show me what I cannot see. Give me ears to hear what the Spirit would say and eyes to see.

Father, I ask that I would be willing and obedient to obey Your will. Help me to hear, not think, but to hear and to obey. I lean upon You, Lord. I lean not on my own understanding, but I trust You with all my heart (Proverbs 3:5-6). I believe You, God. I believe You are who You say You are. I long for unbroken, abiding fellowship with You.

Forgive me and take me to Your heart again. Allow broken fellowship to be restored as I humbly come and acknowledge my need of You. Thank You for Your mercy in the mighty name of Jesus.

THANKFULNESS FOR SALVATION

Father, I'm grateful and I just want to thank You for Your plan of redemption for my life. Thank You, Jesus, for coming for me, for rescuing me, for delivering me, and for being my Savior. I'm so thankful that You did not leave me to myself, but You've given me the Holy Spirit who teaches me and brings forward my new nature in Christ. I'm so grateful for everything You've given me both great and small. With thanksgiving do I give You my praise and the treasure of my heart. You have made me glad and I rejoice in my salvation. I bless the day I was born-again and my name was written in heaven (Luke 10:20). I rejoice that I am Yours and You are mine. I'm so thankful that You chose me. I'm amazed how You love me. And I just wanted to say thank You, thank You, thank You.

MOVING INTO THE PROMISED LAND

Father, in the name of Jesus, I thank You for my deliverance, but I ask for the grace to enter into the land of promise. Break in me anything that hinders me from breakthrough.

I thank You that You have delivered me out of my distress and into a broad place. I ask for the wisdom to enter into this place and to live in a God honoring way. I welcome Your principles and Your wisdom as You will teach me how to do well in the land and to defeat the enemy. I fully submit to You and ask that You would teach me. God, You oppose the proud so I posture my heart by the help of your grace in humility as I learn from You. I ask for a yoke of meekness and lowliness (Matthew 11:28-30), and I acknowledge that I do not know how to live in this broad place. But I know that You are a God of all wisdom and instruction and if I incline my ear to You, You will show me how to eat the good of the land. If I will listen and obey, You will grant me the wisdom to enter in. Help me to occupy and possess Your promises in this new place of breakthrough. Remove from me the old mentality and bring to me the mind of Christ that brings success in this new place. In Jesus' name!

SEXUAL IMMORALITY

Father, in the name of the Lord Jesus Christ I come to You and I repent of my sins. I repent of all sexual immorality. I ask that You would sever any ungodly soul ties between myself and previous lovers (1 Corinthians 6:16). I call my soul out of them and their soul out of me. I ask that You would forgive me of all sexual immorality. I repent of all of my sins and the sins of my ancestors, and I break all curses off of myself inherited from my ancestors (Number 14:18).

I renounce and repent and ask that You would break the curse of fornication, adultery, homosexuality, perversion, pornography, masturbation, orgies, voyeurism, pedophilia, incest, bestiality, rape, molestation, and all sexual immorality in all of its forms (Galatians 5 and 1 Corinthians 6:9-10).

I take authority over any and all unclean thoughts and repent for choosing to be a lover of pleasure rather than a lover of God (2 Timothy 3:4). I command every unclean, demonic force to come out of me in the name of Jesus! Come out of my sexual organs. Come out of my genitalia. Come out of my mind, and my emotions, my memories, and my imagination. Come out of my senses, my mouth, my eyes, and my ears.

I cover my eye gate and my ear gate with the blood of the Lord Jesus Christ and I ask that You would set a guard round about me, that You would show me how to possess my vessel in honor and in holiness (Hebrews 12:14, Isaiah 35:8). Let the blood of Jesus wash clean my mind and my emotions. Cleanse me from every enticing sin and make a way of escape (1 Corinthians 10:13).

I thank You for Your Word that says, "Who the Son sets free, is free indeed" (John 8:36). I declare I am no longer a slave to the lust of the flesh, the lust of the eyes, and the pride of life (1 John 2:16). I ask that You would bring victory so complete in me that it would cause me to echo God's victory, authority, and dominion over my sexuality!

I confess that I am free and that I will not offer my members to be slaves of sin, but I offer the members of my body to be slaves of righteousness (Romans 6:13-16). I decree through the blood of Jesus that I am made holy, that I am godly, and that I am upright before the Lord. I declare that I know how to possess my vessel in a way that brings glory and honor to the Lord Jesus Christ. I will not sin against You, another or against myself with sexual immorality (1 Corinthians 6:18), but I will walk upright and holy by the grace of God, the blood of Jesus, and the cross of Calvary.

PRAYER FOR FINANCES

Father, I thank You that You are Jehovah-Jireh, the Lord God my Provider (Genesis 22:8). I thank You that You meet all of my needs according to Your riches in glory by Christ Jesus (Philippians 4:19). The Lord is my Shepherd, I shall not want (Psalm 23:1). I shall not lack for money (Psalm 34:9). I thank you that, in the name of Jesus, the poverty spirit is broken off of my life. Poverty powers are broken in Jesus' name, because You became poor so I could become rich (2 Corinthians 8:9). I thank You that I'm anointed to prosper.

I am faithful and obedient with my tithes and with my offerings. I thank You for the spirit of wisdom to steward the 90% of my finances (Ephesians 1:17). I thank You that I save money, that I am a lender and not a borrower. I thank You that I'm the head and not the tail (Deuteronomy 28:13). I thank You that I prosper in my finances and I have wisdom. I thank You that I do not overspend, but I operate my finances with self-control (2 Timothy 1:7). I thank You that the wealth of the wicked is laid up for the righteous (Proverbs 13:22). I thank You that You have given me the power to get wealth that I would establish Your covenant in the earth (Deuteronomy 8:18). I thank You that You open the treasury house of heaven

(Matthew 6:20), the storehouse of heaven (Deuteronomy 28:12), and Lord that You supply all of my needs according to Your riches in glory by Christ Jesus (Micah 3:9-10). I thank You that I shall be rich, I shall give to the poor, I shall lend, and I shall give to the needy (1 Timothy 6:18).

I thank You God that money is a tool, that it does not own me, and that I do not love money, but I love God and I love His assignments (1 Timothy 6:10). I use my money for the advancement of the kingdom in the earth to spread the gospel of Jesus Christ. I thank You that You rain down financial blessing upon me and wealth (Ezekiel 34:26). I thank You for radical generosity. I thank You that I am a giver (Luke 6:38), that I give to every need, that I have enough to give to every need and occasion, and that I have seed to sow and bread for food (Psalm 34:9, Acts 20:35).

I thank You that I shall prosper and be in health even as my soul prospers. I thank You for soul prosperity (3 John 1:2). I thank You that there's tens of thousands of dollars in my bank accounts after all of my bills are paid in full. I thank You that I own homes and cars according to my needs and all my taxes are paid in full. I prosper in all things by Your grace (3 John 1:2). I thank You for business deals and favorable opportunities. I thank You that big business accounts come to me. I thank You for favor, the favor of God and man that rests upon my life (Psalm 84:11). I prosper in every area in the name of the Lord Jesus Christ.

I thank You God that I do not take ownership of anything, but I'm a steward of everything and that You have a right to anything You blessed me with (Matthew 21:25). Help me to be a faithful steward. I pray that You would find me diligent and faithful when You return (Matthew 25:29). I thank You that You give me wisdom to know what money is for, and knowledge that my security is in You and not in finances. I thank You that You help me to put it in the right places, that You give me wisdom and discernment, that I would not do business with a crook, that I would have integrity in all of my financial operations, and that I would be above reproach honoring the Lord Jesus Christ and the principles of the Word of God (Romans 12:2).

I thank You that by the blood of Jesus every generational curse of poverty is broken off of my life (Galatians 3:13). I repent for any of the sins of my ancestors if they defrauded anyone or dealt dishonestly with money, I repent of robbing and swindling anyone out of money in the name of the Lord Jesus Christ! The curse is broken and the blessings of heaven flow over my life to the praise and glory of God (Deuteronomy 23:5).

PRAYER OF SALVATION

If you do not yet know Jesus as your Lord and Savior, pray this prayer believing in your heart and confessing with your mouth (Romans 10:9-10), (John 3:16).

Father God, I admit that I am a sinner. I believe Jesus is the Son of God and died on the cross for my sins and rose again. I repent of my sins and ask forgiveness. Jesus come into my heart and be Lord of my life. Thank you that I am now a child of God and my name is written in your Book of Life and I now have eternal life.

MORE RESOURCES

CRUSHING CONDEMNATION—BOOK & COMPANION STUDY GUIDE

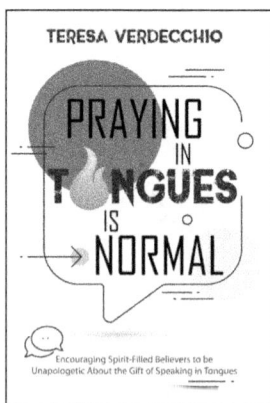

PRAYING IN TONGUES IS NORMAL

To learn more or to invite Pastor Teresa to
speak at your conference or event:

TERESAVERDECCHIO.COM